Make Your Dreams Your Reality
Goal Setting is a Foundation to Success

Joseph K. Edwards MBA, LUTCF

Copyright © 2022 Joseph K. Edwards MBA, LUTCF

All rights reserved. No part of this book may be reproduced or transmitted in any form or by any means, electronic or mechanical, including photocopying, recording or by any information storage and retrieval system without permission in writing from the publisher.

JOKLAN Publishing—Raleigh, NC
ISBN: 978-0-578-36631-9
Title: Make Your Dreams Your Reality: *Goal Setting is a Foundation to Success*
Author: Joseph K. Edwards MBA, LUTCF
Digital distribution | 2022
Paperback | 2022

Dedication

I want to dedicate this book to some of the people who have been important in my life. First, of all my grandparents Joseph & Rosabelle Edwards who never gave up on me. My mother Vonceil Edwards Woodfaulk who was always encouraging me in her own way to go after my dreams. Always telling me "I'm sure you will do it." My wife LaNelle of 43 years for believing in me and supporting my career endeavors and raising our children. We have lived in the Midwest, east coast and now the southern states. She has supported me every step of the way. This is my true soulmate.

I want to thank my business education teacher at Chester High School Mr. Joe Marshall for seeing something in me. I had Mr. Marshall all 3 years of high school and in my senior year he asked me a simple question... Joseph what are your plans after high school? My response was I want to go to college. He gave me a pass to go to the guidance counselor and have the discussion about going to college. The discussion went well and I was a freshman at Cheyney State College that September. The rest is history.

Also, I want to thank my aunt Delores Edwards Mingledoff. She was like a third mother to me. To my brothers and sisters Darrell, Ronald, Rhonda and Kenyetta I give a special thank you for all of your support during the years.

Lastly, my grandmother in law Nellie "Nanny" Laws, my father in law Floyd C. Lewis II and my brother in law Floyd C. Lewis III who was always there to give support and uplift when needed.

Table of Contents

Chapter 1: LV Humble Beginnings 1

Chapter 2: A Scared Man Can't Win 4

Chapter 3: Get Excited About Learning 7

Chapter 4: Always Give it Your Best 10

Chapter 5: Distinguish Yourself from
the Pack 14

Chapter 6: From F Troop to the A Team 19

Chapter 7: Change is a Way of Life 23

Chapter 8: Through Perseverance Comes
Uplift 27

Chapter 9: The Pursuit of Excellence to be
the Best 31

Chapter 10: Everything That Glitters Isn't Gold 34

Purpose

The purpose of this book is to emphasize the importance of goal setting and how it can impact your life. There are times in life in which an individual may choose to dream about what the future can be. Well... there is nothing wrong with that. Dreams can be turned into a reality, but only if you decide to do something about it. You must take action for the reality to set in. There must be an end in sight. Goals should be realistic, written down, shared with someone of importance to you and attainable. They should have a deadline attached to them. I want to accomplish this by this date and time. Your goals need to be revisited with regularity so that they are not forgotten. A goal without action is just a wish. People wish all the time. Disney World is a nice place to go make wishes because it is so relaxing and you have time to make all the wishes in the world. The customer service is so great at Disney they have you wishing you could stay there forever. But, then when you leave the real world returns. If you are a dreamer and have been contemplating the reality of improving your situation then this book is for you. I will share my dreams and how they became a reality. I will share goal setting techniques and how they helped me have high levels of achievement in my career as well as my life. I will divulge what it took for me to start my own company from scratch and become the CEO that I am today. Believe me when I say, that if you want to take your life to the next level, that goal setting can help you get there. But, you must be dedicated to the journey and I can assure it will not come easy.

Chapter 1
LV Humble Beginnings

"From small beginnings come great things"

Back in the mid 1950's I was born at that time in Chester Hospital. Chester Hospital as well as Sacred Heart Hospital were the two premier hospitals in the city of Chester, Pennsylvania where I was raised. The Lamokin Village as it was known was a public housing project located on the westside of the city. We lived on flower street and had access to all of the traffic that came past our neighborhood. LV as it is affectionately known as was a good place to live in the beginning. We had many friends and learned to get along well with each other. Everyone pretty much knew each other and parenting was at its best. Anyone of the parents within a few block radius could discipline you and it was acceptable by your parents with an explanation of course. We learned discipline and respect for our parents and each other.

Even though we were in low income housing I can recall a lot of the adult men and women had jobs. They went to work and came home to take care of their families. I learned at a young age that you had to work. My grandfather, grandmother and mother were the guardians of our household and all three of them worked. When a grown up told us something back then we took it as gospel. We did not question them or talk back. It was forbidden and could lead to a nice butt whipping. There was no such thing as child abuse back then.

I had a nickname given to me back then and it was Big Timer. One of the grownups name Ms. Dean gave me the nickname. When she had a few sips she would always pick on me by saying "Big Timer… The Last of The Big Time Spenders." Now, granite I was about 5 years old when she gave me this name. I believe that she saw something in me that others did not see.

The first school I attended was Booker T Washington Elementary School. This is where all the local children went to school. But, at this school I had classmates that lived in the Bennett Homes Project. We all got along well and was there to begin our educational journey. I started at 5 years old in the 1st grade with no kindergarten experience. I liked school very much as a child and gravitated to learn as much as I could. I admired teachers because they were important people back then and were held to high esteem with the communities in which they lived and taught school.

I learned about domestic abuse at a young age in the Lamokin Village. It would be public news when someone had a disagreement with their spouse. We were so close knit that everybody appeared to know each other's business. But, even in the midst of it all the families stayed together. They knew the importance of keeping the family together and in most cases did just that. I had a challenging experience one day myself as a child. I had received some change from my grandmother and I wanted to get me some rod pretzels. There was a neighborhood store on central avenue that sold penny candy and things of the sort. There were railroad tracks near our house and a path cut down the side of the tracks that we were told to stay away from. I did not listen and decided to take the path to go get my pretzels. I made it to the store safely but, on the way back I encountered three bullies that I did not know. I tried to hide my pretzels but they were older than me and bigger and asked me what did I have? I showed them and they saw the fear in me and took my pretzels and told me to get home. I did not know them and did not ever see them again. I was afraid to tell my parents what had happened because I was told not go near the path or the railroad tracks. That was a valuable lesson I learned and it was to never go on that path by myself. The take away from this was that I did not like the feeling of fear and I really did not like anyone taking something away from me. I was humbled by the experience and this was all a part of the humble beginnings in the LV. We shortly moved out of the LV a few years later but, the friends I made there as a child are friends for life.

Chapter 2
A Scared Man Can't Win

"A Time of Growth and Development"

At this time we had moved from the Lamokin village projects to a nice twin brick home on west eight street. I was eight years old when we moved to this area. I quickly began to make friends and adjust to my new neighborhood. Tree lined streets, a nice big yard next door to our home and a peach tree in the backyard. we had definitely moved on up. I was transferred to Lincoln Elementary school which was four blocks up the street from our home. Once in Lincoln I became a member of the school band playing the cymbals for the marching band. It was pretty exciting to be in the band. Well, as fate would have it my time at Lincoln elementary was short lived. After two years at this school several of the students Including myself became the students chosen to desegregate the schools on the Eastside of the city. I, along with several of my neighborhood friends were bussed to Stester Elementary school and Morton Elementary school respectively. Timeline for this was in or around 1965. At this time I was in the fifth grade when this took place. At first I did not like it But, as time went on I made the adjustment. We were learning things that we were not learning at

Lincoln. The educational atmosphere was different, we had a gym with a stage in it. We could play basketball inside as opposed to going outside in the cold to play. I made the adjustment and began to see the possibilities of what could be if you get your education. I did well at Stetser Elementary to say the least.

As time moved on I went on to Showalter Jr. High School. This was a very important time in my life. The reason is that it was during this time at a blue light neighborhood house party that I met the love of my life. I can recall being at the house party and all of the neighborhood regulars were there as usual. But, it was this shy, cute, redbone just sitting on the steps by herself. She was not interacting with us but she was at the party. So, I asked the host of the party who the girl sitting on the steps was and she said... oh that's Tinkerbell.

I immediately went over to her and introduced myself and asked her to dance. She said yes and the rest was history. Come to find out, nobody was interacting with her because her father was a police officer and a very stern man. I found this out afterwards from one of my close friends. I remember the conversation going something like this... Joe I see you appear to be interested in Tinkerbell. I said yes ... He said be careful with her because her father is the police. That was an (AH HA) moment. Well the reason for this was by this time I had become a member of a neighborhood gang called 7th Street. I wanted this girl and I believed she wanted me. I knew then that A Scared Man Can't Win. I had to meet her father and family if I was to be with her. I met the family and they accepted me. I married the love of my life in January 1978 and we have built a very good life together.

I accepted Islam in 1975 one year after graduating from high school. Islam played an important part in my life because after being a gang member and doing all the things that go along with that. Islam taught me discipline and gave me a spiritual life that I so much needed. This was much needed because my older brother had went into the United States Marines immediately after high school. He and I was in the gang together we had never been separated in life so there was a void that had taken place in my life. We made a vow to each other that he would go serve our country and he made me promise that I would get my education because he was the older brother. I made the promise as he requested. Islam, also gave me a brotherhood of men that was striving to be our best in the eyesight of God. During this time I was in my freshman year at Cheyney State College and the father of two children also. This is where I began to dream about what life could be and the possibilities of getting out of the neighborhood. I had to do better for my children And I realized that getting my education was now my ticket out with the help of God. Allah as we call him in Islam. Imagine going from a gang to the inside of the oldest historical black college (HBCU) in the nation. I knew Allah was watching over me and guiding my path.

Chapter 3
Get Excited About Learning

"The HBCU experience was life changing"

I began my freshman year at Cheyney State College in September 1974. being the first one in my immediate family to go to college was an exciting time for the family and I knew I had to deliver. Everyone was watching me to see how I made out and if I could graduate. I can recall my first day on campus at freshman orientation it was so motivating for me. The president of the college gave the address to the freshmen class and he said... I know you have heard a lot of things about Cheyney. We have good parties and a good time here. but let me remind you that you are here to get an education and that everyone who enters the doors of Cheyney State College does not graduate. He challenged us to focus right then on graduating in four years with our Bachelor of Science degrees. It was at that moment that I committed myself to graduating not just attending college.

My college years were very challenging because I had children when I enrolled and after a good long conversation with my grandfather about attending college. he indicated that we will support you in getting your education but you have to take care of your children too. Well that meant working while being an undergraduate. I agreed and felt I was up to the challenge, I was determined to not let anything get in the way of me graduating from Cheyney. So, instead of living on campus I had to commute to campus every day. The ride was at least forty five minutes to an hour every day I went to class. It was a challenge and a struggle. I went to class during the day and work odd jobs in the evening and at night to do my best to take care of my responsibilities.

The first two years as an undergraduate were exciting but very challenging. I was financially strapped all the time. I was focused on my education but I was beginning to get stressed out from trying to make good grades and make ends meet. Well, I decided that the best thing for me to do was to withdraw from college and go to work full time. I know I was looked at as a failure by some in the family but what they did not understand was I planned on going back and getting my degree. This was just a fork in the road that I had to overcome. During this time I went to work full time at a local hospital. It was a very good experience because it taught me that without an education this was as good as it gets. I worked in the storeroom of the dietary department getting the food out for the cooks to prepare for the patients on a daily basis. I worked at this job for two years and I have no regrets about the decision I was working full time. It was interesting though because when I told my coworkers that I was a college student taking a break to earn some money and would be returning to college most of them sort of shrugged it off and said best of luck with that. It was like it didn't matter because that was their life and it was pretty much as good as it gets.

Well, at the end of my two years working at the hospital it was time to go back to finish my degree. I was a couple years older and a little wiser. But, the commute was different this time. I did not see the commute as a task I saw the beauty in the scenery of getting to campus. I began to look at the beautiful homes and the winding roads on a daily basis and the dream began. I began to dream about living in the suburbs with the single home and my family being able to enjoy their property. I wanted the dog roaming the property playing with the children and having a wife who would appreciate all of this. It was up to me to make this dream a reality and I believed that I could do it but first I had to graduate from Cheyney. During my junior year I married the love of my life, she believed in me. I knew she believed in me and would be there to support my dreams. The dreams were no longer mine, they were ours.

When I went back to finish my undergraduate degree a lot of my classmates had graduated. I saw new faces but the instructors were the same. I knew that it was my destiny to finish college and that I did. Through it all I graduated from Cheyney State College in May, 1980 with a Bachelor of Science degree in Business administration with a concentration in accounting and a minor in management. My goal was to get a position in one of the CPA firms in Philadelphia, Pa and become a CPA. I was focused and had a vision of success. Iqra... read in the name of your Lord.

Chapter 4
Always Give It Your Best

"Winning is an attitude…leave it all on the field everyday"

Now that I had graduated from Cheyney State College I felt that I was ready to take on the world. Watch out world Joe Edwards has arrived. I got employed immediately after college and went to work for Prudential Insurance Company.

I was so excited to get this position as a life insurance agent. I am now a professional was my thought. My hard work at Cheyney had paid off and I was on my way in a career where the sky was the limit. I want to thank Joe L. Sr. for giving me the opportunity. Joe was the district manager of an office located in Brookhaven, Pa. He was a big man with scars around both eyes and large hands. I never asked many questions but one day while I was studying to take the state of Pennsylvania life insurance exam. He walked into the conference room and began to tell me his life story. I found out that he was a professional boxer at one point in his life and that his son was a professional race car driver. But, the take away from him was this…you can make a good living in the insurance industry. Learn to work hard, then smart and always give it your best. This was his advice to me.

Early on I did well with prudential but after a couple years with them they changed the agent contract and went from a debit company to an ordinary company. I could not adjust to the change and decided to leave prudential to seek other employment opportunities. This proved to be a good decision as I sought employment from other companies. By now the CPA dream was about gone. I was in the real world and was determined to make a name for myself.

I went to work for KFC which at the time was a division of PepsiCo. KFC was an interesting part of my life because I went in as an assistant store manager. I thought not bad... let's see where it goes. Well during my five year tenure there I got promoted to store manager. I was known as the person to call when a store was having problems. I was well respected in the tri state area of Pennsylvania, New Jersey and Delaware. I corrected problems in any store and got them back up to par then moved on to the next assignment. But, one day as fate would have it. A few men dressed in suits came into my store and ordered lunch. I asked what type of work that they did and was informed that they were insurance agents. One of the gentlemen was a sales manager and he stayed in contact with me once I told him that I had an insurance license. It was like he would not take no for an answer and was determined to get me on his team. So, after careful consideration and a full discussion with my wife I decided to go back into the life insurance business. This was one of the best decisions that I made in my life pertaining to my career. Joe L Sr. was still in my mind and the success that I saw he had. My goal was to get the job that he had and to live a good life just as he had told me I could do. I was determined to give it my best every day. Within a few months I began a position as insurance agent with United Insurance Company of America with our home office was in Chicago Illinois. One of my goals was one day to get to that home office and see the city of Chicago. The dream was alive and well.

I started in the Drexel Hill district and began to hone my skills as an insurance agent. There were again many season veterans in this office who were doing quite well for themselves. I was assigned a debit in north Philadelphia a place where most agents did not want to go. I serviced this area for a period of three years and established a very good relationship with my clients. I began to make what they call mini trips which would be in Atlantic city or Poconos mountains for a weekend with your spouse. Finally I made my first presidents conference in Acapulco, Mexico. This was so exciting my hard work had paid off and I was now going to a conference to be alongside the best in the country. Once in Acapulco we stayed at the merv griffin resort. This was a fabulous place full of life and excitement, it was so enjoyable and everyone was so friendly. My wife and I really had a fabulous time and I was beginning to consider going to the next level with United Insurance Company of America which would be a sales manager position. With that Being said once the convention was over it was back to business. I was having the time of my life enjoying my work and all the success that was coming along with it.

Chapter 5
Distinguish Yourself from the Pack

"Have faith, believe in yourself and trust your decision"

After returning from the trip in Acapulco Mexico it appears that I was being noticed in my district office. I was putting up good numbers week in and week out. I was dressing the part and I had the professional demeanor to do the job with the best of the guys. But, there was something that I had figured out on my own. If I was to separate myself from the rest of the good agents I had to be different. I had to distinguish myself from the other agents. I began not only to focus on selling and servicing my clients. The difference maker was educating them as to the features and benefits of the life insurance policies that they had been paying for years. Most of the dialog that was taking place in our district meeting was about sales and nothing about education.

Once I took this path and began to schedule weekly policyholder reviews with my clients. The referrals and sales went to another level that I could not have imagined. I knew that the supreme being was guiding my moves and my career path.

Well as fate would have it soon I was approached by the assistant district manager Bob about becoming a sales manager. I said to myself is this really happening? I wanted it but could not be too eager to show how much I wanted the opportunity. I scheduled a meeting with Bob to discuss the opportunity because I had concerns about changing positions. I was comfortable in what I was doing, my income was good and everyone that I saw go into the sales manager position usually came back to the agent position. I know that I was prepared to do the job because again I was a management minor at Cheyney and I looked at this as part of my dream. The five years in management at KFC gave me leadership skills and experience that I needed.

I knew how to work as a part of a managerial team. So, at our meeting I had one specific question for Bob and it was. Bob…why would I want to give up my agency in which I am doing so well and go into a sales manager position in which everyone around me who is a good agent was once a sales manager?

It seems to me that these agents had short term success and I was looking for long term success. Bob said something to me that really got me to thinking and his response was…... Joe do not judge the position by what others have done, You judge the position by what you feel you can make it be. Lots of us have done well in management and he was a testament to that. Good answer I thought…me being energetic and a people person. Also, I have proven to be one of the best agents in the country already. It was time for me to make the decision to take the next step into the role of sales manager. So, after careful consideration and discussion with my wife I schedule a follow up meeting with Bob. This time when we talked I let him know that I was ready to take the next step into the sales manager position. I was thinking that I was going to get a position in my office but little did I know the position was at the district office in the northeast part of Philadelphia. Pa. This was not in the plans and was something to consider because I was being sent to a district office where I did not know anyone and was not doing very well. I knew if I could do well here that it could launch my career to being a district manager the same position that I dreamed of having under the leadership of Joe L Sr. I had to let the district manager in Philadelphia know of my decision within the next few days. Him and I had spoke and he seemed like a good guy and that he had my best interest. I trusted him and that was a valuable lesson learned.

So, I made the decision to take on the position of sales manager in the Philadelphia office. I came in and am fired up and eager to learn my new role as sales manager. I am a green banana ... and when I say green I mean green. The company gave me a lucrative salary to start which lasted six months. But, once I got started in my new role and began to understand the job I realized that the new district manager had lied to me and lured me into a position that was a really bad situation. I was assigned a staff that had seven agencies and four of the agencies were without agents. I went from having total control of my working day to no control at all. The district manager was no help at all and just did absolutely nothing to help me or his district to be successful. I can recall running three open agencies at one time and knowing that one of the other sales managers was working one of my open agencies. But, being an inexperienced sales manager I was focusing on six agencies when I had seven. The district manager again said nothing he just watched me work and began to stress myself out day after day.

I can recall coming home one evening and just lying in my bed looking up at the ceiling and saying to my wife what have I gotten myself into? She assured me it was going to be ok and to just give it my best. She felt my frustration and my anxiety but I had committed and could not go back to my agency. Well, it got more interesting one day when I went into the office one of the sales managers named Gary said to me … Joe I need to talk to you. I said sure Gary no problem, I looked up to this man because his staff was doing very well and he seemed to be a good team player. He often spoke his mind when we had management meetings and would rip into the district manager in an intelligent way but I was not sure why. I soon began to call Gary my big brother because he let me know he had my back. But, getting back to why he wanted to meet with me…we went into the conference room and we sat down and he informed me that he was servicing one of my open agencies and ask me if I was aware of it. I said no because I had not been told he was servicing one of my agencies and as hard as I was working I did not have time to even think about the seventh agency even though I knew it existed. With that being said I told him to give me the agency and that I would service it and he said no. He would not give me the agency to service because he saw what I was going through but he just wanted me to know that he was helping me get through this tough time. He also told me that the district manager is a liar and that is why he is so hard on him in our meeting. Now I had a better understanding of who I was dealing with and that I had to work harder than ever if I was going to be successful and become successful I did.

Chapter 6
From F Troop to the A Team

"If you can believe it, you can achieve it"

The dream is still alive…I am working harder than ever but I am not giving up. I know it's got to get better besides can it get any worse I thought. I am grinding day in and day out with no relief in sight. Then it happens, the district manager gets terminated because of the situation in the office. He is under performing and it has finally been recognized and as a result he lost his job. I felt bad for him of course but at the same time I felt a sigh of relief because this man did nothing to lead the office to success. It appeared to me he was just getting a paycheck and was happy with that. Well, in a few weeks the new district manager John and his brother Joe were appointed to the regional vice president. These men were sharp and they knew the insurance business. I had heard of John and Joe but had never met them, this was the moment of truth. Are these guys the real deal or were they just "good ole boys"?

I can recall having our first management meeting with John and he laid out the plan as to how the office was going to function and ask us to be patient with him and know that he had our backs. As time moved on I am still working hard and one day it happened, I went into the conference room to make some copies and John came in behind me and closed the door. He said Joe can I have a word with you…my response of course John.

Well as fate would have it he recognized how hard I was working and asked me to hang in there with him and not give up. He promised me in that room that we were going to do some hiring and bring in some good people to fill those agencies. He let me know that was one of his main priorities and that it was going to get better. The message was do not give up. I agreed to stay the course and continue to work and trust that we would work together to recruit quality agents to fill these agencies. In the meantime I am learning from Gary and watching his team function like a well oiled machine. This guy is on cruise control and I am out of control. But, that was soon to change.

My staff was known as F Troop. What is F Troop, well it was a television series that was on when I was coming up and it was a group of soldiers in a battalion that could not do anything right. They stumbled over their own feet every opportunity that they got but they never gave up. They kept on trying and the sitcom was funny to say the least.

I used to come home and tell my wife about how F Troop was doing and we laughed just a little about it because again this was my livelihood not television.

John and I kept meeting and now he was calling me Joe E, he knew he had gained my confidence and that I was not going to quit. Now, it begins to happen after about nine months of just surviving here come the recruits. We filled one agency after another with good quality people just as John had promised. His brother Joe had come in to meet me and it appeared for some reason these guys liked me and were looking out for me.

Eventually, I got all of my agencies full and now it's time to show what I can do as a leader and a manager. The following year I felt us gaining momentum. My agents were believing in me and they bought into the idea of being the best staff in the district. My goal now was to be number one and overtake Gary. Seems a little aggressive but I had to focus on being the best and second place would not suffice. By mid-year I felt we were right where we wanted to be making a move to be number one. Bob is in the back of my mind and I hear him saying…do not judge the position by what others did, judge it by what you feel you can do. By year end it happened. This district office under John's leadership in Philadelphia was the number one office in the country, I qualified for the Olympic club and my staff was number one in the office and number seven in the country. We had overtaken Gary and he said little brother I congratulate you on your job well done, you came a long way. Now with this accomplishment I named my staff The A Team. Yes we went from F Troop to the A Team. The A Team was also a television show with Mr. T as a star who could do nothing wrong. These guys were crime fighters who got it right. Now the income was good but more importantly my staff were all making a good income and were proud to come to work. The base team who did not quit on me were three ladies Denise, Karen and Patricia. Denise was a very spiritual lady who would always pray during our staff meetings and told me she was praying for things to get better when they were most challenging and get better they did. The following year promotions were coming to everyone on our team. Being number one came with rewards. John the district manager got promoted to regional vice president, Tony who was the assistant district manager got promoted to the district manager position, Gary got promoted to district manager in a new jersey office and I got promoted to district manager of an office in Southfield, Michigan. Midwest here I come!

The vision I had and the goal that I set back in 1980 to become a district manager finally came to fruition in 1997. Seventeen years later but I never gave up on the dream and always knew I could and would achieve this goal.

Chapter 7
Change is a Way of Life

"Change is inevitable, always be prepared and be open to it"

The motto for Detroit ... "Speramus meliora; resurget cineribus" – "We hope for better things, it will rise from the ashes."

John and I are now best of friends as well as colleagues. He wishes me well and lets me know if we need anything to reach out to him. He still has my back. Our friendship still exists today. When my family and I arrived in Detroit we settled in the suburban area of Farmington Hills, Michigan. We had a beautiful townhouse and was in a quiet suburban community. My office was in Southfield, Michigan and now the work begins.

Upon arriving in my office I was greeted by the secretary that had been there for over twenty years. She was very helpful but, by this being such a large operation she had two assistant secretaries who were also very helpful during my transition. My regional vice president Morrie was headquartered in Chicago and he was very helpful in getting me set up in my office. I was excited and ready to take on the challenge. The Midwest was different. The people were very friendly but I soon found out everyone was not a fan of someone coming in from Philadelphia to take over the office in Detroit. I faced some adversity from within my managerial ranks and had to make some tough decisions but in light of it all. I had an agent named Dennis who was a hard worker and a go-getter. Him and I got to know each other very well and we both soon realized at the conference in Acapulco, Mexico we were both on stage together in a group photo of all the Olympic club awardees. He soon became one of my sales managers and I began to groom him for a district manager position. He had the talent and the work ethic to go places. The footprint for the region I was now in consisted of Ohio, Michigan, Indiana, Illinois and Kentucky. Soon I was traveling throughout the region to different events and meetings. Playing golf as much as I could and enjoying the opportunity that I had to again attempt to make my district number one. There were three district offices that serviced the Detroit metropolitan area and I was proud to have one of them. My office was dead last in the region when I got there but I was not stressed this time because I had been there before when I took my staff. I stayed in Detroit for a period of three years and when I left and returned to Philadelphia due to illnesses beginning to take place within the family with our parents and grandparents this office was in the top 5 in the region. For that I was grateful. I never made it to number one and time ran out on me but it was a heck of an experience for a young man from Chester, Pa getting this opportunity was a blessing. During my time there as I indicated earlier one of my goals was to get to Chicago and visit our home office. Well, it happened when Morrie invited me to meet with him in Chicago and we had dinner in the Prudential Plaza which is one of the largest skyscrapers in the city of Chicago. The next day we went to the home office on Wacker drive and I met the president of the company and some other corporate executives. Joe Edwards was again being recognized for a job well done in the Midwest. The takeaway is that I set the goal to get to Chicago early on when I was hired with United Insurance Company of America and I believed that I would someday go there to handle the business of the company and once more that dream and vision became a reality. Goal setting was the key and having a plan got me there. Change is inevitable and those who cannot adapt to change soon find themselves falling by the wayside. You have to get comfortable being uncomfortable in order to achieve success. I can recall as a teenager going to work for the youth corps in the city of Chester. There were only so many summer jobs to go around and we met at a place called the Opportunity Center to get your job assignment.

There was an older man named Mr. Watts, a light skinned man well-dressed bald on the top and hair on the sides of his head. He got on stage and told us this and I quote... "When I call your name and I give you your job assignment that is where you go. I do not want to hear you live on the westside or eastside of the city. Do not come to me asking for a change in your job assignment because you are not working in your backyard. Everyone cannot work in their backyard."

Well he must have been speaking directly to me because throughout my corporate career it seems that

I never had the opportunity to work close to home, but I always remember the words of Mr. Watts and I always reflected on that day in the Opportunity Center during my career. Welcome change, adapt and adjust, have faith and good things will happen for you.

Chapter 8
Through Perseverance Comes Uplift

"Love of family is so important, spend the time with them because
Once they are gone you cannot make up for it"

Now that we are back home, I have made a career change from district manager to sales manager in Philadelphia. I had to regroup, look myself in the mirror and ask myself what is the next move. I did not know but what I did know is that our families were so happy that my wife and I were back home. I felt so much love and outpouring coming from them.

Even though it was a step back in my career, it was a step forward in my life because at that time I felt that our families needed us. Shortly after coming home it began where death was beginning to hit the elders of the family. I soon realized that I did not belong anywhere but where I was. I had been battling a disease of the colon for many years and taking medication for it and now that I am back home the illness seems to get even worse. The good thing was that I had my family to support me as I began to fall victim to an illness called ulcerative colitis.

After about twenty four months I had to have surgery to have my large intestine removed. This was a series of three surgeries total that spanned 18 months. The illness really took a toll on my health and I found myself disabled for a period of time and trying to figure out what I can do to keep myself focused and motivated. I decided at this time that a mind is a terrible thing to waste and that it was time to go to graduate school to pursue my Masters Of Business Administration. I realized that it had been exactly 20 years since I received my bachelor degree but I felt now was the time and even though I was down I was not out.

I entered a twenty four month Masters of Business Administration (MBA) program at Wilmington University in New Castle, Delaware. The vision along with the goal was to get this MBA and get back into the workforce. Once embarking on this endeavor and beginning to enter class I realized that I was one of the few individuals in the classes with gray hair. I immediately accepted the challenge to compete with the younger students and tried to learn as much from them as they did from me. It was a good fit and worked out well. But, this quest did not come without its challenges due to my poor health. I found myself in and out of the hospital during the two year period. I was having flare ups of the colon and it got so bad that my wife felt the stress I was under and asked me to give up on pursuing the MBA for the time being until my health got better. She felt the stress of going back to school and my age along with my health condition was too much. After a lengthy discussion about this she agreed to support me in my quest to finish this two year program on time. I can recall at one point I took a final examination while hospitalized. I contacted the instructor and told her I was hospitalized and asked if she would let my daughter come to the campus and get the final and I could take it so that I would not fail the class or have to take an incomplete.

She knew how hard I was working and she agreed to send the final to me by my daughter. Well, I received the final and can recall walking down the hall with my hospital gown on, iv bottle and stand in tow and my final. I went to one of the family rooms and lost myself in the mental quest to pass this final and finish this class. In the meantime the nurses came to check on me and I was not there. It was a panic because they thought I had left the hospital. Everyone was looking for me…it seems kind of funny now that I look back on it but when I surfaced after taking my final the nurses came in my room and there I was. When asked where I was, I replied that I had to take a final because I am attending graduate school. They thought it was kind of silly of me to go do what I did and mentioned that I am a patient and that I should be more concerned about my health at this time. I took it on the chin and smiled.

I finished the MBA program on time and set a good example for my family to never give up.

Well as things began to get better my health was improving and the family was stable for now, I had to decide my next move. So, I decided that at this time it would be a good idea to go into the banking industry. I can work inside and it would be less stressful than going back into the insurance industry. I went to work as a financial consultant for a well-known bank and then worked as a branch manager. Banking was interesting because now I had a chance to become more well-rounded as a business professional and would be able to help individuals to get the banking products and services that they needed. But, after three years in banking my health was much better now I decided that it was time to go back into the insurance industry and finish my career. I joined Monumental Life Insurance Company and went into their MBA fast track program to again get back to the level of district manager. Now I find myself working in New Jersey and the commute was about an hour long every day to the office but I was okay with it.

I believed that this was a good opportunity for me and that this is where I belonged.

Also, remember Mr. Watts said everyone cannot work in their backyard...

Within a twelve 18 month period I had shattered the goals of the program and was promoted to the position of Branch Manager in Atlantic City, New Jersey. Through perseverance comes uplift!

Chapter 9
The Pursuit of Excellence to be the Best

"The Best is Yet to Come, Be a Believer"

Atlantic City, New Jersey is one of my favorite places to vacation and now I am working here. What a dream come true. I found myself taking my lunch breaks and walking on the boardwalk in Atlantic City just thinking how wonderful life is. This was a time in my life that changed the game for me and the team that I had will never be forgotten.

The team in the Atlantic City office were like no other. These men and women were seasoned veterans who knew their job and were good at it. After getting to know them and getting to work with each of them the dream came to me that we can be number one in the country. I shared this vision with the team and they bought into it and besides who does not want to be a part of a winning team. The beginning of a new year was coming and our goal was to come out swinging for the fence.

That year we all worked hard and long. I found myself when the weather was bad just getting a motel room and staying there overnight or a couple of nights if necessary so that I could get to the office and be with these guys. We became like a family and were there for each other. We worked like a fine tuned machine and we were not going to lose focus of our goal to be number one. Along with being the best came perks and money. Our incomes were good and more importantly our families were being well taken care of. Each of us had our own personal goals but as a team we were focused on being the best. One of my agents Ed and I used to go to breakfast together on a regular basis because he got to the office early and so did I. But, Ed was a former district manager and was from New Jersey as well as being a pastor of a church and I can recall that day that he told me Joe we are going to deliver on being number one I can feel it. My reply was Ed. I sure hope so but along with that he said we are also going to make a good income along the way. I let him know how much I appreciated working with him and having him and his wife as a friend.

As fate would have it, there were not a lot of ups and downs in this office due to the experience of the team and their maturity. In the end we finished the year as the number two branch office in the country. There was a seasoned manager and team in Chicago who won out over us. I was a little disappointed but as a team we had one hell of a year. Everyone was well paid for their efforts and I was happy for each and every one of my agents because we gave it our best. I learned a valuable lesson from this office and it was that if you believe you can be the best that's half the battle. The other half is execution. Once this year ended I got promoted to a large district manager. Now I am headed to Raleigh, North Carolina. I have been assigned to lead the office in Raleigh and Greensboro, NC. I am getting older now and my wife and I both agreed that this would be the last move for us and that we would retire in North Carolina. As the lord would have it I spent ten years exactly back home with the family but again I was needed in another part of the country to share my skills with the folks there and to help give back to the community in which I would be living.

"When you have a dream you have to grab it and never let go"

Chapter 10
Everything That Glitters Isn't Gold

"I did it my way and never had to say to myself…what if!"

I arrived in North Carolina on a cold January morning. I recall feeling alone and missing my wife and children but this was the decision that I made. I had to step up and get on with the business at hand. Anyone who is contemplating relocating to another part of the country for employment opportunities needs to really evaluate the pros and cons of the decision. Talk with those who you care about, pray on it and then make the decision. I have no regrets about the decisions I made because I had thought it through and my wife and I knew what we expected the end result to be. So, as I began to work in the offices after a little time I noticed something very different from my team in Atlantic City. Many of the workers here were not committed to a career in the industry. Most of the employees were just looking for a job and were passing through. Turnover was high and this area consisted of a highly educated population that was seeking other types of employment but would accept a position as an insurance agent until the position that they were really seeking came to be.

My Regional Vice President asked me to promise him after I took the position that I would not retire before him and I gave him my word that I would not do that. He was a company man from Tennessee who was really nice and professional and he was someone who I did not mind working with. As fate would have it, one year after I committed to David the company did some restructuring of the RVPs and he was out of a job. We talked and he indicated that some things were going on internally at his level that he would not agree to and felt that it was best if he resigned. I was somewhat disappointed that this is the man who brought me here and now he is gone after twelve months. Well what was on the horizon was a merger with a new company. I had never been a part of a merger during my tenure in corporate but everything I had heard about a merger consisted of people losing their jobs and folks getting hurt.

Once the merger took place everything that I had heard about mergers became a reality. Many of the district managers who I had worked with in New Jersey were seasoned veterans of the business and very successful to say the least were let no longer with the company for whatever reason. Moral was low among the managers and the company came in like gangbusters to say the least. The attitude was our way or there is the door. I looked at the situation one evening while attending a leadership conference at SeaWorld in Orlando, Florida. The culture of the organization changed overnight and the president of our company gave his last speech at this conference.

The new regime was in full effect and was flexing their muscles at every turn. During my career I had attended many of these types of conferences but this one was unique. People were scared for their jobs and were afraid to talk to anyone about their feelings because you did not know who to trust. My wife and I after the awards dinner was over that evening went back to our suite and had a discussion about what we saw and felt. We talked about my future in my current position. The bottom line was that I was not going to let these people turn me back or control me as an individual. I did my job but the company was not going to control my life. I knew that night it was survival and that the goal for me was to get to retirement. That was my personal goal.

I soon found myself given an option to go back to Philadelphia with all expenses paid.

I refused the offer and told these individuals that I came to North Carolina to retire and that was what my wife and I were going to do. I found myself after this meeting working in a sales manager capacity which was fine with me because I knew if I took the sales manager offer I would be able to retire comfortably. Some of my colleagues in New Jersey were not so lucky. Being in corporate is like playing a game. It is a game of personalities who likes you who makes the decisions and being in the right circle along with the right place at the right time. I was seasoned and knew how to play the game. It was not about them, it was about me and my future. I knew that I could ride it out as long as I wanted to because I was that good at what I do.. Time was on my side as well as God! I knew I was protected from those who meant no good and that I just had to practice patience.

I remained as a staff manager for a few years and did well but my mind was not at ease. I had begun not to enjoy coming to work. I always told myself that when coming to work is no longer enjoyable then it's time to go. I prayed on my situation and made a decision to get out of management and to finish my career as an insurance agent. This was the best decision I could have made. As a manager I could not see the forest for the trees. I was a corporate man and was doing everything I could to make the company better in spite of how we were being treated. As an agent I led my district in sales until the day I retired. I retired on top of my game (#1) and everyone was surprised when I announced my retirement. But, as fate would have it once the trees were removed the dream, vision and goal was to start my own insurance agency. Yes, if I could do this now with all of my experience in managing offices across the country I would become CEO immediately and my fate would be in my own hands.

Being connected as a member of Omega Psi Phi Fraternity, Inc. is a blessing for me. I have friends in high places and had the connections to coach me as to what I needed to do to start my own company. I had a meeting with a friend and he was already successful as an independent agent and he agreed to show me how to get started and to mentor me as long as I needed it. Besides, who better to show you how to get started in a business than the person who has already done it and is doing it at a high level. We came up with a scheduled plan as to when we were going to meet and what steps that I needed to take prior to every meeting until its completion. At completion the goal was for me to open my agency and work for myself. When I retired from the company I was working for I was asked what I was going to do and I simply replied…I am going to work for myself. I was wise enough to begin the execution of my strategy to create my own business prior to retiring and keep everything under wraps until its completion. I am proud to write that Edwards Insurance LLC was created and opened for business in 2015 and I retired from my company in 2017. My plan was executed to perfection. "When God is on your side, it does not matter who is against you."

To this day Edwards Insurance LLC is a thriving business. We have several solid business relationships and our footprint expands in SC, NC & PA. Never let anyone tell you how to live, your job is just that. Dream big, dream often and never give up.

A dream is really a vision of what can be, but bringing that dream to a reality is totally up to you. Surround yourself with people who support your vision and let go of the dream killers. Dream killers are everywhere. Know when to walk away and when to stay. Do not make decisions out of anger... be patient... think things through and stay in control of your destiny and one day you may be a CEO also.

I remember being in Philadelphia at a Harold Melvin and the Blue Notes concert and these guys were putting on a very good show that evening. But, if you know anything about Philadelphia there are a lot of talented musicians there and this particular evening there was a man who wanted to come on stage and sing with the band. I remember Harold Melvin saying, "Let him come on and join us... there is always room for one more". The man was Teddy Pendergrass.

Ikhlas or Purity (of Faith)

Say : He is God, the One and Only:

God, the Eternal, Absolute;

He begets not, nor is He begotten;

And there is none like unto Him

The Holy Quran

About the Author

Joseph Edwards is a resident of Raleigh, North Carolina. He is married to the love of his life LaNelle. He is a loving father of 5 adorable children who he loves and admires so much. Joseph retired in June 2017 from Transamerica Premier Life Insurance Company to pursue his dreams of entrepreneurship. With that being said and the blessing of the Supreme Being. I started Edwards Insurance Agency LLC in June of 2015. When asked by my peers what I was going to do when I retired my response was build my own business and do as much community service work as I can't help others. Joseph has over 30 years experience in the insurance industry.

Joseph is an active member of Omega Psi Phi Fraternity Incorporated and Prince Hall Free and Accepted Masons. He accepted Islam as his religion in 1975 and has been an active member and true believer since associating himself with the religion of Islam.

He was the recipient of numerous awards during his working years. Also have received several community service and fraternal awards. He has been instrumental in developing scholarship programs within organizations to help underprivileged children get into institutions of higher learning.

Joseph is a graduate of Cheyney State College class of 1980 which is now Cheyney University of Pennsylvania. He received a Bachelor of Science degree from Cheyney with a concentration in accounting and a minor in management. He also received his Masters of Business Administration degree from Wilmington University located in New Castle Delaware class of 2004. With a concentration in managerial leadership.

In my spare time I enjoy golfing, riding my Harley Davidson, reading a good book and spending quality time with my family.

www.ingramcontent.com/pod-product-compliance
Lightning Source LLC
Chambersburg PA
CBHW032018290426
44109CB00013B/708